Wild and Woolly
MERINO SHEEP

Rosaura Esquivel

PowerKiDS press™

New York

Published in 2018 by The Rosen Publishing Group, Inc.
29 East 21st Street, New York, NY 10010

First Edition

Editor: Theresa Morlock
Book Design: Rachel Rising

Photo Credits: Cover (background) Keith Levit/Design Pics/Getty Images; Cover, pp. 4,12, 22 Eric Isselee/Shutterstock.com; Cover, pp. 1, 3, 4, 6, 8, 10, 12, 14, 16, 18, 19, 20, 22, 23, 24 (texture) Kira Volkov/Shutterstock.com; p. 5 John Carnemolla/Shutterstock.com; p. 6 Evgeny Litvinov/Shutterstock.com; p. 7 (Jacob) Gabor Tinz/Shutterstock.com; p. 7 (Merino) patjo/Shutterstock.com; p. 7 (Corriedale) UnknownLatitude Images/Shutterstock.com; p. 7 (Leicester) NatureAndCities/Shutterstock.com; p. 9 CatJB/Shutterstock.com; p. 11 Baronb/Shutterstock.com; p. 13 aaltair/Shutterstock.com; p. 15 Richard Lyons/Shutterstock.com; p. 16 Orxan Rzayev/Shutterstock.com; p. 17 Steve Lovegrove/Shutterstock.com; p. 18 Valentin Ivantsov/Shutterstock.com; p. 20 A_riakhin/Shutterstock.com; p. 21 Kseniia Perminova/Shutterstock.com.

Cataloging-in-Publication Data

Names: Esquivel, Rosaura.
Title: Merino sheep / Rosaura Esquivel.
Description: New York : PowerKids Press, 2018. | Series: Wild and woolly | Includes index.
Identifiers: LCCN ISBN 9781538326039 (pbk.) | ISBN 9781538325339 (library bound) | ISBN 9781538326046 (6 pack)
Subjects: LCSH: Sheep–Juvenile literature.
Classification: LCC SF375.2 E87 2018 | DDC 636.3–dc23

Manufactured in the United States of America

CPSIA Compliance Information: Batch #BW18PK: For Further Information contact Rosen Publishing, New York, New York at 1-800-237-9932

CONTENTS

Wonderful Wool

For thousands of years, people have raised sheep for wool. Wool is the fine, soft, wavy or curly hair that forms the coats of sheep and other animals. People shear, or cut off, this wool and make it into cloth. Since **ancient** times, wool has been prized for its warmth and **durability**.

Merino sheep produce some of the highest-**quality** wool in the world. Their wool keeps out wetness and doesn't itch as much as other types of wool.

Sheep were **domesticated** by 5000 BC.

Domesticated Sheep

All modern-day sheep are **descended** from two wild species, or kinds, of sheep: mouflon and urials. People **developed** different breeds, or types, of sheep through selective breeding. Selective breeding means bringing together male and female animals with wanted features so that they'll have babies.

Some sheep are kept for meat. Sheep meat is called mutton, so these breeds are known as mutton-type sheep. Breeds that are kept for their wool are called wool-type sheep.

mutton ⟶

Wool-type breeds are sorted into groups based on the kind of wool they produce.

Merino sheep

Corriedale sheep

Leicester sheep

Jacob sheep

A Royal History

During the Middle Ages, the wool trade was a major **industry** in Europe. The Spanish developed the Merino sheep breed sometime during the 1100s. The royal Merino flock of Spain was famous for its high quality.

At the end of the 18th century, people first took Merino sheep to Australia. By 1810, Australia was home to more than 30,000 sheep. Today, Australia is the leading producer of Merino wool. Australian Merino wool is the highest quality sheep's wool in the world.

Fuzzy Features

Before 1700, selling or trading Merino sheep to countries outside of Spain was punishable by death!

Each year, Australia produces more than a quarter of the world's wool.

Types of Merinos

There are four main groups of Australian Merino sheep—Peppin, South Australian, Saxon, and Spanish. There are other groups of the Merino breed in different countries. The Delaine Merino was developed from the Spanish Merino and is popular in the United States in areas such as Texas and Ohio.

Merinos are sorted into groups based on the length, type, and quality of their wool, as well as their ability to **thrive** in certain **environments**. Merino sheep do well in hot, dry conditions.

Fuzzy Features

There are about 34.2 million sheep in New Zealand. That's seven sheep for every person!

Merino sheep are very strong and usually live long, healthy lives.

Sheep Basics

Male sheep are called rams, females are called ewes, and babies are called lambs. Ewes usually give birth to one to three lambs at a time. Sheep reach adulthood when they're about a year old. Most sheep live for about 12 years. The oldest known sheep was a Merino who lived to be 23!

Sheep are herbivores, meaning they only eat plants. Merinos eat grass and other low-growing plants. Like all sheep, Merinos have a four-part stomach.

Fuzzy Features

Sheep can recognize people and other sheep. They're able to remember up to 50 other sheep faces for up to two years.

Sheep have many predators, including coyotes, bears, and foxes.

13

Shearing Sheep

Merinos need to be sheared regularly to avoid health problems. Shearing is usually done during the spring. It's important for shearers to be very careful because Merinos have soft skin that can be cut easily. To complete shearing as quickly and safely as possible, most shearers follow a set pattern on the sheep.

In Australia, Merinos are usually sheared in barns called shearing sheds. Thousands of sheep are moved through these sheds throughout the season. Today, electric shears allow shearers to cut wool faster and closer to the skin.

Fuzzy Features

As of 2016, the sheep-shearing world record was 731 ewes in nine hours! The record is held by shearer Matt Smith of New Zealand.

Wool is sometimes called fleece.

The World's Woolliest Merino

In September 2015, one Merino sheep became famous. A hiker was taking a walk through the Australian wilderness when they spotted a shocking sight: a huge, overgrown sheep! Rescuers believe Chris the sheep left his flock about five years ago and had lived in the wild ever since.

Chris had many health problems because of his bushy coat and needed to be sheared at once. Ian Elkins, an Australian champion sheep shearer, removed 89 pounds (40.4 kg) of wool from Chris.

Merino wool →

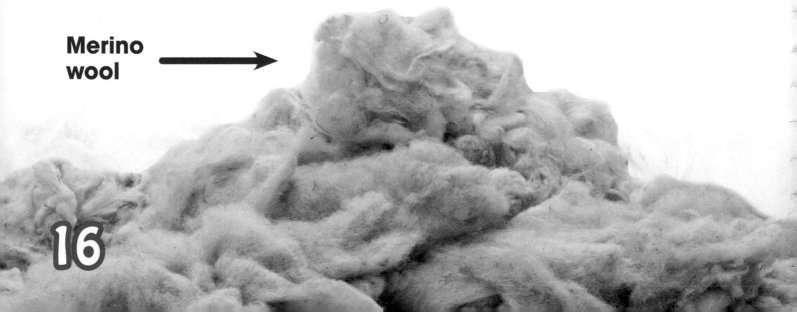

The wool that was sheared from Chris holds the world record for the most wool removed from a sheep.

Processing and Spinning

After the fleece is removed, it's cleaned to remove dirt and lanolin, a kind of natural grease. Lanolin is used to make makeup! Next, the fleece is carded. Carding straightens the tangled pieces of wool and lengthens them.

Spinning is the process by which wool is made into yarn. Large-scale spinning is done on machines. However, many people spin wool at home. Merino wool is some of the softest and finest wool in the world. It's also very springy.

Fuzzy Features

A single Merino hair is three times finer than the average human hair!

Natural Merino wool is usually bright white.

A Fashion Favorite

Merino wool is soft, light, and breathable, which means air can flow through it. Although wool is usually thought of as a cold-weather cloth, Merino wool is often used for spring and summer clothing. It's sought after because it can keep the wearer warm during cold seasons and cool in hot ones.

Today, Merino wool is often used to make sportswear. Its springiness allows it to bend with the wearer's body and its breathability keeps sweat at bay. It's even flame **resistant**!

Merino wool clothing can be both stylish and comfortable.

Marvelous Merinos

A single Merino sheep produces between 6.6 and 13.2 pounds (3 and 6 kg) of wool each year. These animals are sturdy, gentle, and easy to take care of. They're able to live in environments where conditions may be as hot as 95° Fahrenheit (35° Celsius) or as cold as 5° Fahrenheit (-15° Celsius).

Merinos are very special sheep. Since the time of their development, people all over the world have prized the wool they produce. Today, the popularity of Merino sheep and their wool continues to grow!

GLOSSARY

ancient: Very old, from a long time ago.

descend: To come down from a source.

develop: The act of building, changing, or creating over time.

domesticate: To breed and raise an animal for use by people.

durability: The ability to stay strong and in good condition.

environment: The conditions that surround a living thing and affect the way it lives.

industry: A group of businesses that provide a certain product or service.

quality: A degree of excellence.

resistant: Having the power to resist.

thrive: To grow successfully.

INDEX

WEBSITES

Due to the changing nature of Internet links, PowerKids Press has developed an online list of websites related to the subject of this book. This site is updated regularly. Please use this link to access the list:
www.powerkidslinks.com/wandw/merino